# Space

100 QUESTIONS & ANSWERS

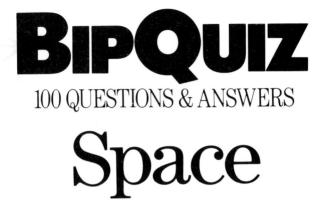

# BipQuiz

## 100 QUESTIONS & ANSWERS

# Space

*Illustrations by Bruno Heitz*

**Sterling Publishing Co., Inc.  New York**

10  9  8  7  6  5  4
Published by Sterling Publishing Company, Inc.
387 Park Avenue South, New York, N.Y. 10016
© 1994 by InfoMedia Communication
English translation © 1994 by Sterling Publishing Co., Inc.
Distributed in Canada by Sterling Publishing
% Canadian Manda Group, P.O. Box 920, Station U
Toronto, Ontario, Canada M8Z 5P9
*Printed in France - Publiphotoffset, 93500 Pantin*
Sterling ISBN 0-8069-0937-4

# How to Use the BipPen

The BipPen must be held straight to point to the black dot.

Point to a black dot.

●

A continuous sound (beeeep) and a red light mean that you've chosen the wrong answer.

Point to a black dot.

●

A discontinuous sound (beep beep beep) and a green light mean that you've chosen the right answer.

Keep your BipPen for our other books.

# Headings

Each question belongs to a specific heading.
Each heading is identified by a color.

**Conquest and exploration**

**Planets and satellites**

**The solar system and the universe**

**Names and dates**

**Various**

1

T he sun represents over 99% of the solar
system's total mass, which also includes:

5 planets          ●

9 planets          ■

15 planets         ▲

2

T he solar system's 9 planets, from closest
to farthest from the sun, are: Mercury,
Venus, Earth, Mars, Jupiter, Saturn, Uranus,
Neptune, and:

Minerva          ●

Meteor           ■

Pluto            ▲

**3**

The alternation of day and night on earth is due to the fact that the earth rotates:

on its own axis ●

around the sun ■

around the moon ▲

**4**

Since it has many apparent similarities with earth (white polar caps, seasons, rust color), Mars has often entertained people and their discussions and fantasies of:

little green men ●

the mining of Martian iron ■

Comets are blocks of ice a few miles (kms) in diameter whose path is far from the orbit of the sun. Some get closer to the sun and heat up: The surface ice changes into vapor and forms a streamer known as the:

ribbon    ●
scarf    ■
tail    ▲

The sun and its planets formed around 4.6 billion years ago, after a huge explosion, from a cloud of gases and dust. This formation is the theory of the:

Big Crunch    ●
Big Bang    ■
Nihilo    ▲

Venus is not the planet closest to the sun, but it is the warmest because it retains solar energy. Its atmosphere mostly contains clouds of carbon dioxide and:

oxygen ●
hydrogen ■
sulfuric acid ▲

Like the moon, Mercury is covered with craters caused by the collision of solid objects with it. These scars remain on the surface and cannot be erased because of the lack of:

atmosphere ●
human presence ■
sunlight ▲

The *Voyager II* probe flew over Uranus in 1986 and Neptune in 1989. These planets both have:

many satellites

a single satellite

a single common satellite

Without the sun giving us its heat and light, there would be no life on earth. The sun is at the center of the solar system and is:

a planet

a satellite

a star

Pluto is both the smallest planet of the solar system (⅕ the size of Earth) and the farthest out (40 times farther from the sun than Earth). Pluto's name is that of a(n):

god of antiquity ●

astronomer ■

ore ▲

The energy produced by the sun comes from hydrogen fusion. The sun's rays measure:

6250 miles ●

62,500 miles ■

437,500 miles ▲

The universe is so huge that astronomers have their own measuring unit, the light-year. It measures the distance covered by light in a year, or 5938 billion miles (9500 billion km). Light travels at a speed of:

187,500 miles/minute ●
187,500 mph ■
187,500 miles/second ▲

Arab astronomers advanced new ideas in medieval astronomy, while Europeans remained faithful to Ptolemy's theories. Which one of these three words is of Arabic origin?

star ●
zenith ■
eclipse ▲

Under some particular conditions, the density of a star's core is so great and its gravity so strong that it retains light. These stars are called:

aberrations ●
super-dense ■
black holes ▲

The sun's electric particles sometimes come into contact with the earth's atmospheric gases and light them up. At the South Pole this phenomenon is called the aurora australis. At the North Pole, it's called the:

aurora polaris ●

aurora borealis ■

aurora nordicus ▲

Planets rotate when they turn upon themselves, and they revolve when they turn around the sun. It takes the earth a year to achieve a complete revolution and it takes Pluto:

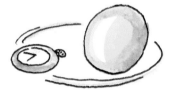

6 months ●

1 year ■

247 years ▲

If the American space shuttle reaches a speed of 17,500 mph (28,000 km/hr) when it orbits around the earth, it lands at a speed of:

219 mph
625 mph
6250 mph

Since the moon has no atmosphere, it also has no:

sound
sun
temperature

The first American spaceships were so small that astronauts had to fulfill which of the following requirements?

be contortionists ●
not measure over 5'11" ■
not wear shoes ▲

From the earth, a solar eclipse occurs when the moon blocks the sun. The moon is then found:

between earth and sun ●
on other side of the sun ■
on the other side of ▲
the earth

Meteorites are rocky fragments that penetrate the earth's atmosphere. They're incandescent while travelling through it, and they become:

comets ●
shooting stars ■
black holes ▲

The word galaxy comes from the Greek word *gala,* meaning *milk*. The Greeks believed that the Milky Way came from the milk spilled while the goddess Hera nursed a child who later became famous for his twelve labors:

Hercules ●
Achilles ■
Oedipus ▲

In his novel *From the Earth to the Moon*, Jules Verne has his characters leave earth in a:

rocket ●

balloon ■

artillery shell ▲

In the 17th century, Isaac Newton articulated the principle of universal gravitation, which states that every mass exerts a force of attraction. He got the idea after watching:

the tides ●

an apple fall ■

a sunset ▲

The first rockets, whose remains date back to the 13th century, were small metallic cylinders propelled by powder. They were developed by:

the Egyptians ●

the Chinese ■

the Russians ▲

Although medieval man imagined a rocket propelled by the gas created by the combustion of two liquids, it was a modern American, R. Goddard, who made the first such device. This rocket reached an altitude of:

40 ft. (12 m) ●

330 ft. (100 m) ■

3300 ft. (1000 m) ▲

The earth revolves around the sun. By rotating upon the earth's axis, day and night are determined. Nonetheless, we always speak of sunrise and sunset, with the sunrise occurring in:

the west ●
the east ■
the north ▲

On October 4, 1957, an R7 rocket put the first artificial satellite into orbit around the earth. The name of the satellite was:

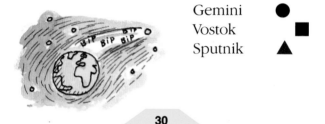

Gemini ●
Vostok ■
Sputnik ▲

The Soviets were the first to send a living being into space in 1957. Its name was Laïka and it was a:

dog ●
frog ■
monkey ▲

On April 12, 1961, the Soviet spaceship *Vostok I* took off with the first man to orbit the earth. His name:

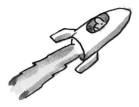

Yuri Gagarin ●
Leonid Brezhnev ■
Samuel Korder ▲

On July 21, 1969, a man from the *Apollo 11* mission walked on the moon and exclaimed, "That's one small step for a man, one giant leap for mankind." This quote was made by:

Neil Armstrong ●
Michael Collins ■
Edwin Aldrin ▲

The *Apollo 17* mission, of December 1972, was the last! At the end of this mission, how many men had walked on the moon?

4 ●
12 ■
14 ▲

The conquest of space also includes some tragedies. The space shuttle *Challenger* exploded after less than 2 minutes of flight and with 7 astronauts on board. Missions were interrupted for:

2 weeks ●
2 months ■
2 years ▲

T he Soviets, who lost the race to the moon, concentrated their efforts on the first space station designed to be inhabited on a permanent basis. Its name:

Saliut ●
Soyuz ■
Korkov ▲

S cientists who study the sky and the planets are called:

meteorologists ●
astronomers ■
spatiologists ▲

B ruce MacCandless was the first man to walk in space outside his spaceship without a link to his craft, thanks to:

a flying chair ●
an adjustable helmet ■
a flying carpet ▲

O ur knowledge of the solar system's farthest planets has progressed considerably thanks to which space probes?

*Jupiter* ●
*Voyager* ■
*Viking* ▲

Venus and Earth are the two brightest planets. Venus' atmosphere reflects over 70% of the sunlight it receives. In relation to Earth, it is:

closer to the sun ●

farther from the sun ■

equidistant from the sun ▲

Around March 21 and again around September 21, the length of the day and night are the same everywhere on the globe. These two days are called:

equinoxes ●

latitudes ■

midseason ▲

E xploration missions allowed us to see the moon's hidden surface. Indeed, we always see the same side of the moon from the earth, since, in relation to its revolution around the earth, it rotates on its axis:

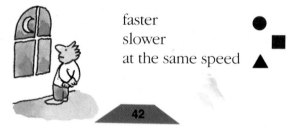

faster ●

slower ■

at the same speed ▲

T here are huge volcanoes on Mars, the red planet. The largest has an altitude of 89,000 ft. (27,000 m) and a base that spreads over 375 miles (600 km). Right now, these volcanoes are:

extinct ●

active ■

dormant ▲

Asteroids are celestial objects that fly around the solar system. Apparently, they come from small bodies that haven't solidified into planets. The largest known asteroid has a diameter of:

330 ft. ●

0.625 mile ■

625 miles ▲

The Meteor Crater came from a huge meteorite with a 165 ft. (50 m) diameter; it weighed over 65,000 tons. The crater is found in:

Arizona ●

Australia ■

China ▲

The solar system's giant planets are surrounded by rings composed of billions of particles less then ¼₄" (one mm) wide. Galileo discovered Saturn's rings in the:

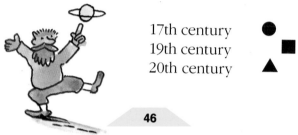

17th century ●
19th century ■
20th century ▲

The two *Voyager* probes that flew past Jupiter allowed for the discovery of something that had been invisible from the earth:

clouds ●
rings ■
volcanoes ▲

The ancient Greeks believed that when the star Sirius appeared at dawn, with the sun, there would be a heat wave. These hot spells now carry the name given by the Romans to the constellation Sirius (*Canis Major*):

dog days ●
drought ■
aridity ▲

The theory according to which "time must be considered a dimension similar to the three others (length, width, height)" is from:

Asimov ●
Einstein ■
Hawkins ▲

The Americans alone have sent men to the moon. The space research and development program is administered by a governmental agency known as:

FBI ●
CIA ■
NASA ▲

S pace has been a subject of international conventions. If new planets are discovered they are to be the property of:

the first people there ●
all of humanity ■
the USA ▲

M ost meteorites that cross the atmosphere burn themselves out before landing on earth. Some do reach the earth's surface, though. How many fall in an average year?

100 ●
1000 ■
10,000 ▲

In the 2nd century B.C., Eratosthenes calculated the earth's circumference, and despite a few errors, he came to a close approximation:

3125 miles (5000 km) ●
6250 miles (10,000 km) ■
25,000 miles
  (40,000 km) ▲

In the 3rd century B.C., Aristarchus of Samos was the first to think of the sun as the center of the universe. This theory is known as:

hereticism ●
heliocentrism ■
gravitationalism ▲

In 1543, the Polish astronomer Copernicus placed the sun at the center of the universe. He also established the duration of the earth's revolution around the sun and rotation upon its own axis, but was mistaken as to:

the shape of orbits ●
the planets' order ■
the sun's diameter ▲

Kepler (1571–1630) was the astronomer who proved that the planets' orbits weren't circular but:

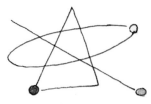

elliptical ●
triangular ■
diagonal ▲

G alileo, an admirer of Copernicus' theses (sun as the centre of the universe), was forced by the Catholic Church to:

recant his own opinions ●
prove his own opinions ■
convert ▲

O ne theory states that dinosaurs disappeared because of a brutal change in the earth's climate, after a huge cloud of dust was created by the earth's collision with:

the moon ●
a meteorite ■
another planet ▲

S o that all people in all countries can read them, the names of stars on celestial maps are usually marked in:

English ●
Latin ■
Greek ▲

A day is the amount of time that a planet takes to rotate on its axis. A day lasts 24 hours on earth, but on Venus it lasts:

12 hours ●
3 days ■
243 days ▲

A number of civilizations have considered the sun a god. The sun was the most important divinity in ancient Egypt and it had the name:

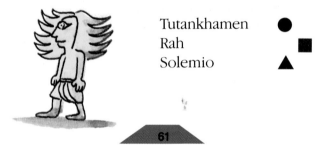

Tutankhamen ●
Rah ■
Solemio ▲

The earth takes 365 days, 5 hours, 48 minutes and 45 seconds to revolve around the sun. Since the calendar year has only 365 days, one day is added every four years. This is known as a:

double year ●
leap year ■
voluble year ▲

When it is summer in the Northern Hemisphere, it is winter in the Southern Hemisphere. The demarcation line between the two hemispheres is called:

the equator ●

the tropic ■

the axis ▲

The moon revolves around the earth at the same speed as it rotates upon its axis. This is why we always see the moon's same side, which looks different at different times of the lunar cycle. Between the new moon and the full moon, there are:

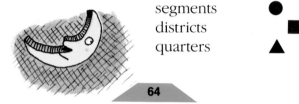

segments ●

districts ■

quarters ▲

In 1929, the astrophysicist Hubble observed that galaxies were spreading in all directions across space. This is why the universe is said to be:

close to the end ●

expanding ■

exhaling ▲

N owadays, artificial satellites play a part in our daily lives, especially in telecommunications and:

> meteorology ●
> energy ■
> science fiction ▲

W hen an astronaut is on board his spaceship orbiting the earth, centrifugal force equalizes the force of the earth's gravity and the astronaut floats. This condition is:

> weightlessness ●
> levitation ■
> cognition ▲

D ue to the lack of gravity, men and
women in space:

feel better ●

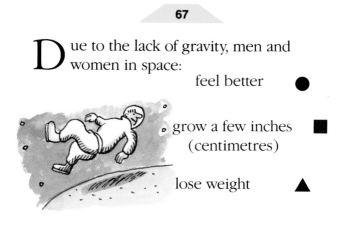

grow a few inches
(centimetres) ■

lose weight ▲

D uring their lunar mission on *Apollo 11,*
Aldrin and Armstrong left behind a
number of tools so that, with the help of a
laser, they'd be able to:

measure earth / moon distance ●
take pictures ■
recharge their batteries ▲

S tars are extremely hot balls of gas that shine from their own light. They transform their principal gas, hydrogen, into another gas:

oxygen
carbon dioxide
helium

T he main planets have secondary planets, known as satellites. The solar system's 9 planets all have natural satellites except for Venus and:

Mercury
Saturn
Jupiter

P lanets with atmospheres owe their color to the chemical composition of that atmosphere. Oxygen gives Earth its blue tint, and particles of ferrugineous sand give Mars its color:

yellow ●
white ■
red ▲

I n order to compete with American rockets and shuttles, the Europeans have created a rocket named:

Europa ●
Ariane ■
Saturn ▲

Venus was long thought to be a star, and it served as a marker in the heavens. Its brightness is due to its proximity to the sun, and the fact that it reflects so much of the sun's light. The planet's name is that of the goddess of:

light ●
beauty ■
day ▲

The moon's gravity is ⅐ that of the earth, so that 220 lbs. (100 earth kgs) weigh how much on the moon?

6.6 lbs. (3 kgs) ●
66 lbs. (30 kgs) ■
33 lbs. (15 kgs) ▲

The earth's oceans and continents rest on large rigid plates that move quite slowly. Volcanic eruptions and earthquakes occur when these plates:

collide ●

separate ■

turn around ▲

B y capturing the light and heat from other astral bodies, radiotelescopes can deduce what the temperatures of other planets are, and which gases are found in their atmospheres. The largest telescope in the world can see the light of a candle from:

31 miles (50 km)　●

625 miles (1000 km)　■

15,000 miles
(24,000 km)　▲

O bserving the moon apparently allowed prehistoric man to establish the first calendars. Traces recovered of such calendars include groups of 28 to 30 notches etched in:

rocks　●

bones　■

skins　▲

N<small>ASA</small> started building the space shuttle in 1972. This rocket-plane lifts off like a rocket and lands like a plane. The first flight took place in:

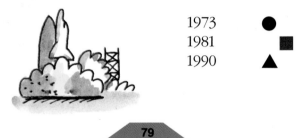

1973    ●
1981    ■
1990    ▲

T he earth's rotation has many secondary effects. Since its centrifugal force diminishes from the equator to the poles, the same person weighs more:

at the poles    ●
at the equator    ■
at the tropics    ▲

Water occupies ⅘ of the earth's surface and accounts for what percentage of its weight?

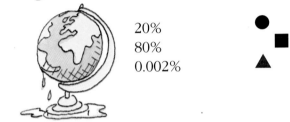

20%
80%
0.002%

If the universe is limitless, its expansion that started with the Big Bang will last forever and all matter will transform into:

energy
water
antimatter

Whether natural or artificial, a satellite is an object that revolves around another. The moon is a satellite of the earth, and the earth is a satellite of:

the sun
Jupiter
Mars

Even in space, satellites don't completely escape from gravity, which is why they move around the earth:

in an orbit
in a straight line
in parallel formation

Rockets must burn huge quantities of combustible fuel in order to be launched. They must carry oxygen along with them, whereas regular planes find it in:

gas ●

the atmosphere ■

their reserve tanks ▲

Ariane, the European rocket, is regularly sent into space to put satellites into orbit. Ariane is usually launched from French Guiana, from:

Pointe-à-Pitre ●

Kourou ■

Canaveral ▲

Without gravity, some metals can be forged together to produce new materials that are both light and sturdy. These experiments are carried out by:

probes ●
satellites ■
astronauts ▲

The outside walls of artificial communication satellites are covered with solar cells. These capture the sun's rays and provide the satellites with:

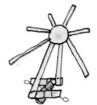

electricity ●
humidity ■
water vapor ▲

S atellites travel along a special orbit about 22,500 miles (36,000 km) above the equator. Since they rotate at the earth's speed, they appear immobile. This is why they are called:

irreducible ●

geostationary ■

abandoned ▲

W hen observing the sky, one can see that some stars form patterns. We call such patterns constellations. In a single year, the earth passes before the twelve constellations that form:

the zodiac ●

the horoscope ■

the magma ▲

T he Bayeux tapestry, which dates from 1077, shows the Saxon king of England in 1066 observing a comet. At the time, seeing such a comet was considered a bad omen. Indeed, the Saxon king was killed in 1066 by:

William the Conqueror ●
Charlemagne ■
Charles Martel ▲

When Americans performed their several explorations of the moon, they used a:

go-cart ●
dune buggy ■
lunar module ▲

To build their first multistory rockets, the Americans were inspired by the German World War II rockets, known as:

V-2s ●
panzers ■
tanks ▲

I f they weren't protected from it, spaceships would burn when going through the atmosphere. Their protections are called:

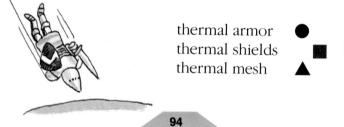

thermal armor ●
thermal shields ■
thermal mesh ▲

A rtificial satellites unfurl solar panels and antennae in space. So as to protect delicate tools from the heat of the sun, they are covered with Mylar, which is made of sheets of:

aluminum ●
silver ■
gold ▲

The astronauts' lunar footprints will never go away, because of the lack of air on the moon. When Neil Armstrong put his foot on the moon, how many people were watching the event on television?

3 million ●
100 million ■
600 million ▲

The shuttle is equipped with a large external tank that holds the liquid hydrogen and oxygen for the rocket's engines. This reservoir is the most important component of the shuttle. The shuttle has how many components?

millions ●
dozens ■
hundreds ▲

Valentina Tereshkova was the first woman to fly in space, in:

1933 ●
1963 ■
1983 ▲

The sun gives heat and light, which is why it has often been considered a god. The Greeks represented the sun as a young male god flying across the sky in a fiery chariot. His name was:

Apollo ●
Nero ■
Horus ▲

H alley's comet is named after the British astronomer who studied it. He predicted that it would return every 76 years. In 1835, it took the shape of:

a sword

a hammer

a basket

100

I f we live in a closed universe, the theory of general relativity predicts a phenomenon opposite to the Big Bang (expansion). This contraction would be the black hole at the end of the world, and is named:

Big Brother

Anti-Bang

Big Crunch

# Stars & Constellations

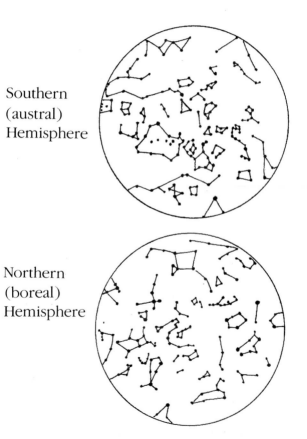

Southern
(austral)
Hemisphere

Northern
(boreal)
Hemisphere